# Isabella's Shoe Studio

Read! Doodle! Create!

A DOODLE STORYBOOK

Text and Art by Violet Lemay

duopress

*(The little © and the word "copyright" mean that the book idea belongs to the company that created it: Duo Press, LLC.)*

*(This is the date this book was created. Think about this as the book's birthday!)*

*(Charla, the book's designer, is like a magician. She puts everything together and makes the book look beautiful!)*

*(Blah, blah, blah…Ok. Seriously. Nobody can copy this book to sell it or to build a paper house. If somebody does that, without asking nicely, we will put him or her in time-out.)*

Book design: Charla Pettingill

*(Elizabeth helps to make the pictures nice and crisp!)*

Illustration Assistant Extraordinaire: Elizabeth Kidder

*(Well, First Edition means that this is the first time we've made this book. If we make some changes and do it again, we call it Second Edition.)*

First Edition

*(This number is unique, or exclusive, to this book. Every book has a unique number so anybody can find the book easily. ISBN means International Standard Book Number. This is good anywhere, from Argentina to Alaska.)*

ISBN: 978-1-938093-18-0

*(This is the country where you can find the factory where this book was made. It also means that the book has spent more time on a boat crossing the ocean than the person who wrote it. Strange, isn't it?)*

Printed in China

*(This is our address in cyberspace where you can see more of the fantastic books we have for you.)*

duopress
www.duopressbooks.com

*(This little square is a Quick Response Code. It can take you to our address in cyberspace very quickly if you use a smartphone. If your phone is not smart, send it to school, or just type www.duopressbooks.com.)*

# Isabella's Shoe Studio

is a **Doodle Storybook.**

This means that this is a book
in which you can
**read a story,** *story!*        **doodle** fun stuff,
and create your own
**art,** all at the same time!

On each page you will discover something
about a super-creative girl named **Isabella** and her **shoe studio.**

(That's her saying "Hi" below!)

Also, each page gives you a chance
to **color, design,** and **draw** your own artistic creations.
**Isabella** has also prepared a few fun games
and activities where you can **create your own studio,**
doodle shoes in **a crazy feet gallery,** and **collaborate**
with your parents, your best friend, or whomever
you want!

Are you ready?     *Doodle!*
*Create!*
*Go!!*

**Hi!**

My name is Isabella Ivory Edleston–Finch, and I am eight years, seven months, three weeks, and four days old.

I am an artist.

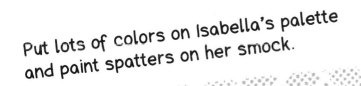

Put lots of colors on Isabella's palette and paint spatters on her smock.

When I grow up, I will have a studio in New York City, like the fabulous Kate Spade.

Dress Isabella like Lady Liberty.
Don't forget her pointy crown!

My dad says it's no wonder that I am an artist because my mother is an artist, and so is Nana (my grandmother). My little brother Leo wants to be an artist, too.
We'll see about that.

Mom and Dad

Nana

Tam and Leo

Draw your family in these pictures.

Nana's art is fashion. She <u>designs</u> all kinds of dresses.

(Underlined words are explained at the end of the book.)

Dresses

Nana's Dresses

Fill the window with beautiful dresses.

All of the ladies who work in Nana's shop sit in a circle
to finish up the hem on every gown that she designs.
Nana says I'm still too little to help sew hems,
but she says I sort beads better than anybody.

Finish up the beading on this wedding gown.

My mother is an artist like Nana,
but Mom is a hat designer.
She makes her hats in Nana's shop
and sells them there, too.

Design a hat for Isabella.

Mom and Nana draw millions of hats and dresses,
and then they make their favorite drawings
into a <u>collection</u> of real hats and dresses.

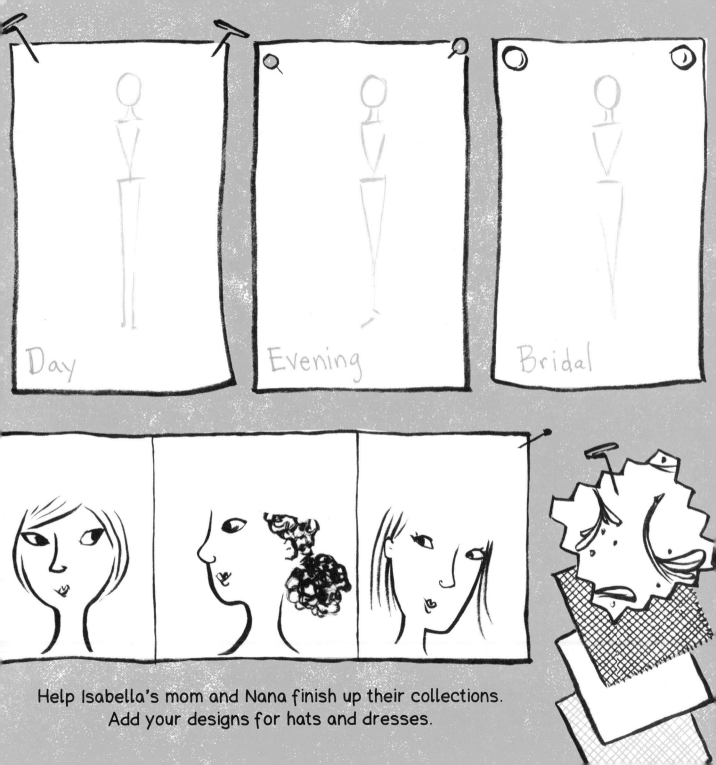

Day

Evening

Bridal

Help Isabella's mom and Nana finish up their collections.
Add your designs for hats and dresses.

Sometimes I help. I haven't made a whole dress yet, but I am getting really good at making hats.

Design a hat for yourself!

I love drawing dresses like Nana,
and I love drawing hats like my mom.

Sweater dress →

Purse

flowery SCARF →

Fabulous Boots

Sailor hat

Flats?

Beachy SANDALS!

Design the perfect dress and hat for each <u>outfit</u>.
Don't forget shoes and handbags!

I paint landscapes because I love grassy hills,
and cows make me laugh...

Draw sheep and cows and ducks and chickens all over this farm.

...and I love drawing cityscapes.
Leo always adds tall buildings called <u>skyscrapers</u>.

Who lives here? Draw people and their pets looking out of the windows.
Help Leo add skyscrapers behind the apartment buildings.

But what I really, really, really, REALLY love to draw are shoes: fancy shoes, comfy shoes, city shoes, and country shoes. I think about shoes all day, and I dream about shoes all night!

How about you? What is your favorite thing to draw?
Draw it here!

When I was a baby, my favorite pair of shoes had puppy paws on the bottom. My little brother Leo wore them when he was a baby, too.
Mom said all babies can wear puppy shoes—girls or boys.

Baby shoes are fun to design because babies are silly, and they will wear anything!

Help Isabella design a bunch of baby shoes.
Make some that are sweet, and some that are funny!

Now my favorite shoes are moccasins. When I wear them, I am Pocahontas. I wish Leo would pretend with me, but he would rather play with blocks.

Isabella's moccasins will be much prettier after you have drawn a beaded bird on top.

What do your favorite shoes look like? Draw them here.

At school I wear the brown
Mary Janes I got from my cousin
Charla. She's too big for them now.
I like wearing Charla's
hand-me-downs because
when I wear them,
I think of her.

Plus, these Mary Janes
have rubber soles
so I can play kickball
at recess. I am better
at second base than
anyone else on my team.
We call ourselves
the Bottle Rockets.
The Rockets need me,
and Charla's
Mary Janes!

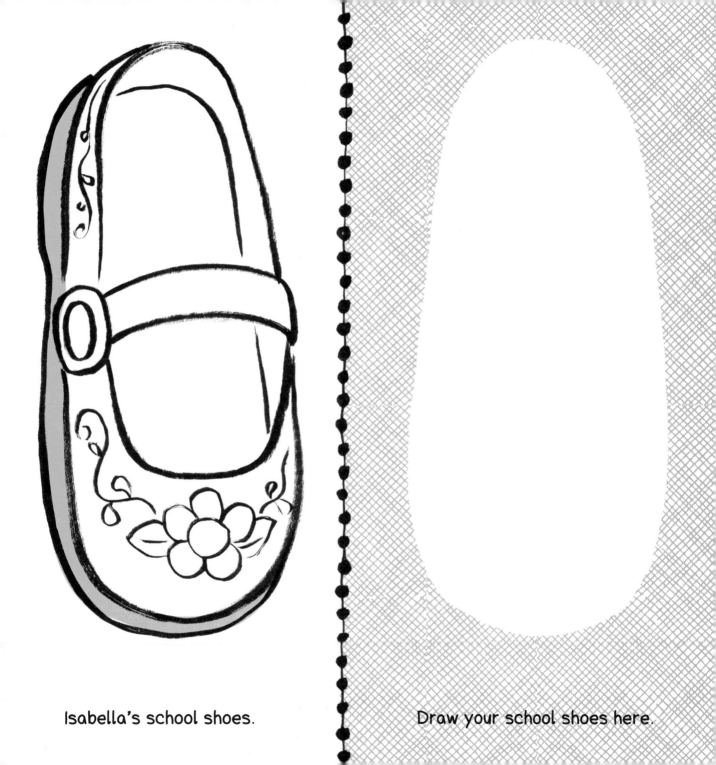

Isabella's school shoes.

Draw your school shoes here.

My best friend Lilia has green shoes with a bow on the strap. Sometimes we trade.

Lilia's Shoes

Isabella's Shoes

Draw Lilia's shoes on Isabella,
and Isabella's shoes on Lilia.

lilia

isabella

Draw your best friend's shoes here.

In dance class we wear toe shoes, tap shoes, and ballet flats.

Isabella's dance shoes are missing their ribbons and bows.

My teacher, Madame Eva, is always telling me,

Isabella, extend, extend! Your <u>spine</u> is a strand of pearls.

Mom told me what she means: "Stand up straight, and stretch!"

Now it's your turn: stand up and s-t-r-e-t-c-h!

For parties, I have shiny pink flats with a flower on the toe. Nana wears kitten heels, and Mom wears high–high–HIGH heels.

Nana's kitten heel

Isabella's flat

girl's party shoe

Mom's high heel

platform heel

mule

**Color all of these shoes with bright colors for the party and learn their names!**

Draw your party shoes here.

Let's play a game:
I'll design shoes
for everyone to wear
to a fancy party,
and you design
the clothes
to go with
the shoes.

You're invited
to the party, too!

Tam

Leo

You!

Lilia

Isabella

Dad

Mom

Nana

Dress everyone for the party.

# On **museum days,**

I wear comfy
walking shoes.

Draw your most comfy
shoes here.

I also carry a notebook
because museums
fill my head with ideas—
especially the paintings.
They <u>inspire</u> me.

Fill these empty frames with art.

I turn my ideas into shoes.

What inspires you today? Draw it on this sneaker.

Sometimes, I turn my ideas into...

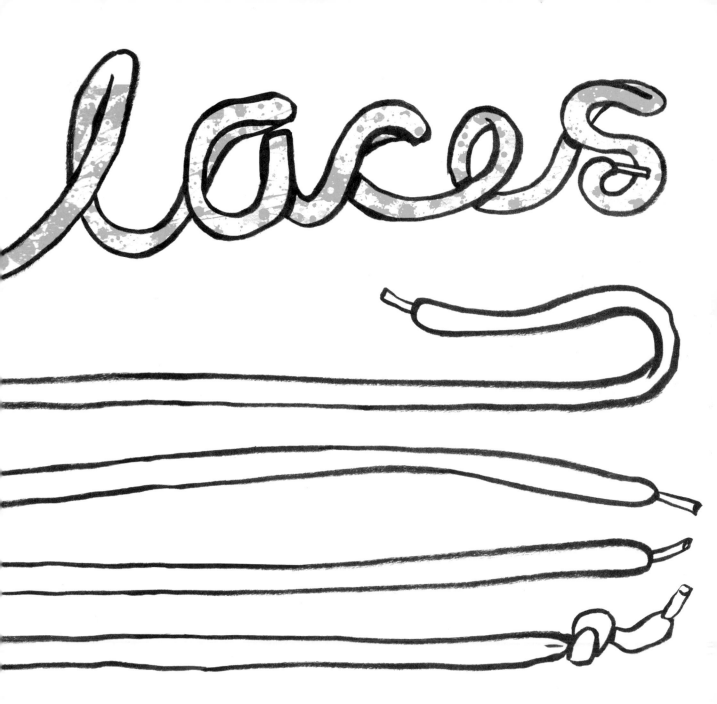

Decorate these shoelaces with your ideas.

Not all of my shoe ideas are for girls and ladies.

**Boys' shoes** are fun to draw, too.

**When my dad** gets home from work he unties his laces and says,

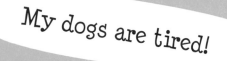

My dogs are tired!

Fun Fact: This shoe is called a WINGTIP, or BROGUE.

Dress up this shoe for Isabella's dad.

Shoes that light up
make me happy,
even on cloudy
days.

Use a white crayon
to draw tiny lights on Isabella's shoes.
Make them flash as she taps her feet!

I designed light-up shoes for my dad to wear to work so that his office will really sparkle!

Draw sparkly shoes on Isabella's dad.

When the seasons change, we can wear different kinds of shoes! I love designing summer shoes, especially flip-flops with diamonds that glitter.

Decorate these flip-flops,
and paint the girls' toenails to match!

**Rain boots** are super fun to design.
I have a whole book full of rain boot ideas!
Mom calls it my **rainy day book.**

We thought Leo would fill his rainy day book with buildings, but he has other things to do when it's wet outside.

Leo's
RAINY
day book

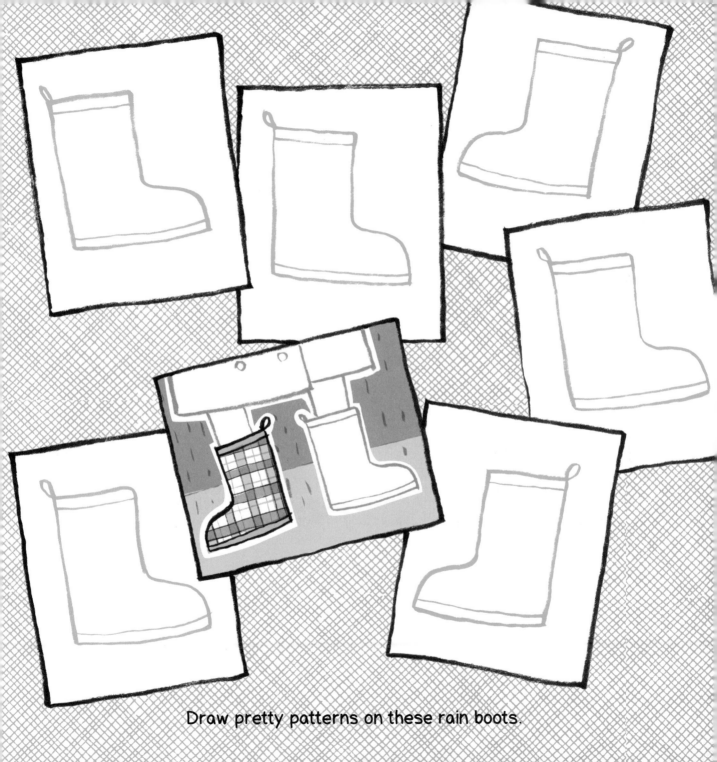

Draw pretty patterns on these rain boots.

Snow boots are fun to design, too...
and they are lots of fun to wear!

Draw snowflakes all over this page.
Remember, no two snowflakes are exactly alike!

Design some cute snow boots that will keep your feet toasty warm!

I don't always wear
**shoes.**

When I'm reading,
I like to wear
just my **socks**
so I can curl my toes
around each other
and think.

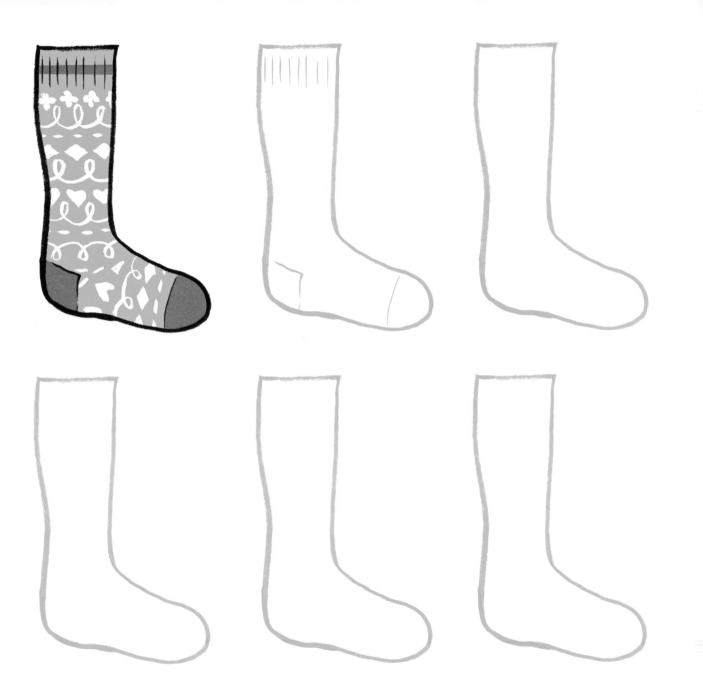

Design beautiful socks for Isabella to wear.

Sometimes I read books about shoes.

Draw covers for these books.
Make sure to include your favorite books!

## Audrey Hepburn

was a famous actress
with great style.
When she wore flats
in a movie called *Sabrina*,
ladies everywhere wanted
to wear flats like her.

Color these flats all different ways: solids, plaids, zebra stripes, polka dots, flowers, etc. Draw buckles and bows on the toe of each shoe.

# Marie Antoinette

was the very last
queen of France.

Way back then, only kings
and queens were allowed
to wear high-heeled shoes,
and they painted the heels
red to make them fancier.

That made the people
in the kingdom very,
very angry. They got rid
of Marie Antoinette and the king
and passed a law against
high-heeled shoes.

See how important shoes can be?

Shoes can change history!

Cover Marie Antoinette's dress with pearls and the prettiest lace you can imagine, and color her heels red!

In *The Wizard of Oz*, **Dorothy** wore magic slippers that protected her from the Wicked Witch of the West.

Quick, the Wicked Witch is coming!

Dorothy needs her magic slippers. Make them extra shiny!

I don't like wicked witches, but I do like the **boots** they wear.

In fact, I think I'd rather wear black boots than sparkly slippers.

Design a black boot for Isabella.

Pioneer

Cowgirl

Biker

What should Isabella wear with her boots?

My mom likes to say that every pair of shoes has something to say. These are my **friendliest** shoes.

Let's

play!

Design some more friendly shoes here.

What do these shoes say to you?

I like shoes that are <u>dainty</u> (and so does Nana),
but sometimes it's fun to wear shoes that are tough.

My mom says,

Sometimes designers give girls' names to the shoes they make.

Vikki*

Anya

Marcia

Coco

isabella

Charla

Paz

Cecilia

Design shoes named for you and your friends.

Of course, it's not good to have too many shoes.
Twice a year we all go through our closets
and pick out some nice ones to pass along
to people in need.

Fill this basket with all of the shoes that Leo and Isabella
are too big to wear anymore.

There are many places where you can donate your shoes.
For more information on donation centers see the end of this book.

Sometimes we keep the boxes, though. Nana, Mom, and I collect beautiful shoe boxes for storing special things like bits of ribbon, and markers, and sketches torn out of notebooks.

Decorate these boxes for all of the shoes you have designed.
Make sure to include your name!

Nana gives notebooks to my mom and me (and Leo!)
so that we can keep our ideas safe.
This morning I got an idea for a new shoe,
and I drew it in my notebook.

Help Isabella fill her notebook.
What other ideas come from this breakfast table?

Artists get ideas from everything they see.

Do the stars and moon give you
an idea for a shoe?
If the night sky were a shoe,
what kind of shoe would it be?
Draw your idea in the bubble

I pin my ideas to a board, just like my mom and Nana.

Eiffel Tower flat

Butterfly Party Shoe

detail

Giraffe Boot

Taxi Sneaker

CAB

starry night
wedge

daisy flip-flop

Finish up Isabella's idea board with your own ideas.

Sometimes we all like the same idea, and we share it.

"Sunny Day"

Nana

Mom

isabella

Draw yourself wearing the Sunny Day collection.

I love working with Mom and Nana. Maybe someday when I am a famous shoe designer we will all have a shop together.

What will you be when you grow up?
Draw yourself here, all grown up!

There are millions of things to do in a studio.
You could design dresses, or toys, or buildings.
You could plan cities, or make science experiments.
You could sing, or dance, or play a violin.

(Your Name)

(Your Studio's Activity)

Studio

Fill these pages with your ideas.

Fill these pages with your ideas.

Fill these pages with your ideas.

Fill these pages with your ideas.

Artists and designers
are always looking
for inspiration.
Everywhere you go,
be on the lookout
for all kinds of shoes!

Use the following pages to draw
the craziest shoes that you see.
Include your own designs, too!

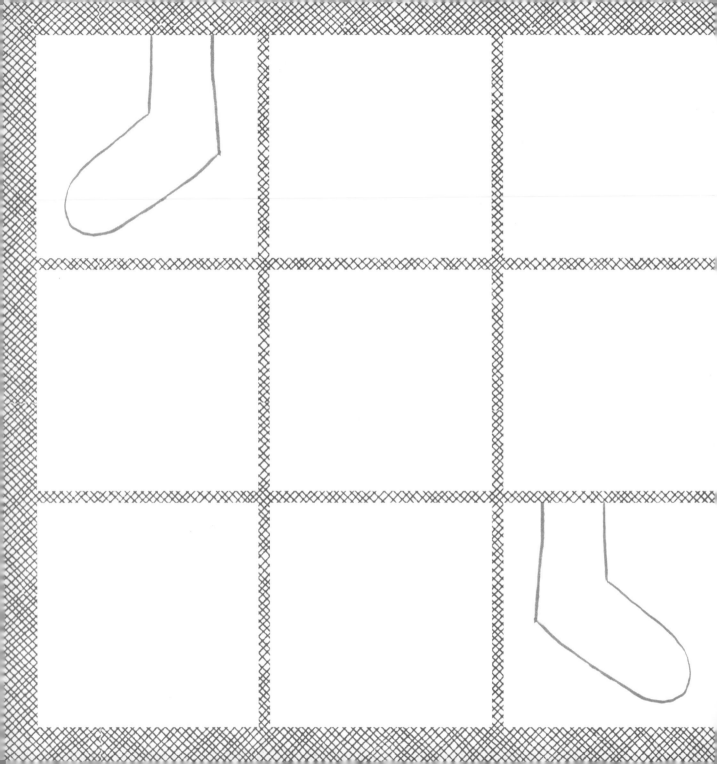

What inspires you?

"Bee" creative!

Sometimes artists work *together.* In other words, they <u>collaborate</u>. Use the following pages to collaborate with your friends and design some amazing shoes together, as a team!

Our Man's Shoe Design

Our Team's Party Shoes

Design patterns for the shoes in these pages.

# Design Team
# Project: Boots for Tam

Design boots for Tam so he can play in the snow!

Ruff!

Draw everyone's ideas on this page.

Our Team's Boots for Tam (and all Dogs!)

Hey, we're not finished yet! You can *play* with shoes.

Shoes are like people—every pair of shoes has its own <u>personality</u>, and every pair of shoes makes you feel a little different when you wear them. That's why it's fun to try on shoes!

Play the **shoe dress-up game** with your friends.

All you need is a bunch of old shoes. It's fun to add some other <u>accessories</u>, too, like hats and scarves and handbags, and it's good to have a mirror so you can see how you look in your crazy new shoes.

Once you have everything on, it's time to be an actress! Imagine who might have bought those shoes, and pretend to be that person.

# Cool New Words

*(for artists, designers, and pretty much anybody who likes to get smart!)*

**accessories** |ak-sess-uh-rees|: A small item, such as a belt, scarf, or hat, worn to make clothing more beautiful or complete. *With this accessory, your outfit will be complete.*

**bad attitude** |bad| |at-i-tood|: A bad mood or frame of mind. *That crabby person has a bad attitude.*

**collaborate** |co-lab-o-rate|: To work together with other people. *My friends and I like to collaborate on projects.*

**collection** |ku-lek-shuhn|: A group of new clothes made by a designer, all at once. *I love every dress in this designer's summer collection.*

**dainty** |dayn-tee|: Small and delicate; ladylike. *The china teacup is very dainty.*

**design** |di-zine|: To draw something that could be built or made. *The artist likes to design chairs.*

**inspire** |in-spire|: To give someone a new idea. *Let's go to the museum; I need something to inspire me.*

**outfit** |out-fit|: A set of clothes worn together. *Your new belt looks nice with that outfit!*

**personality** |pur-suh-nal-uh-tee|: The qualities or traits that make a person unique. *She has a fun personality.*

**skyscraper** |sky-skray-pur|: A very tall building with many stories. *Her office is at the top of that skyscraper.*

**spine** |spine|: The row of bones going down our backs. *It feels good to stretch my spine.*

# Shoe Donation Sites

There are many places where you can donate your shoes.

For a list of these places, and how you can help people in need, visit our website at www.duopressbooks.com/isabella.help or scan this QR code.

CPSIA Compliance Information: Batch #041513DP For further information contact Duo Press, LLC at info@duopressbooks.com